reflections

Thoughts Worth Pondering
One Moment at a Time

John Blackwell

Foreword by Jaime Blackwell

New York

reflections
Thoughts Worth Pondering One Moment at a Time

ISBN 978-1-60037-578-1

MORGAN · JAMES
THE ENTREPRENEURIAL PUBLISHER

Morgan James Publishing, LLC
1225 Franklin Ave., STE 325
Garden City, NY 11530-1693
Toll Free 800-485-4943
www.MorganJamesPublishing.com

In an effort to support local communities, raise awareness and funds, Morgan James Publishing donates one percent of all book sales for the life of each book to Habitat for Humanity. Get involved today, visit **www.HelpHabitatForHumanity.org.**

To

Shirley Leggett

Ken and June Jennison

With Gratitude

Foreword

By Jaime Blackwell

For most of my life, I've been listening to my father talk about the things in this book. They represent the ideas that he has tried to teach my brother David and me. They also represent the ideas by which he tries to live.

One of the things that my dad doesn't talk about in this book is that the Blackwells all ended up in Salina, Kansas, through an extraordinary set of circumstances. One of those circumstances is that I not only introduced Dad to Salina, but I also introduced him to Ken and June Jennison. As providence would have it, June is a trustee of Kansas Wesleyan University, where my father serves as Dean of the Chapel. And Ken is in charge of public service at KSAL, the oldest radio station in Salina. Ken has worked for KSAL longer than my dad has been alive!

From time to time, my dad and I have both been interviewed on KSAL. Ken and Dad hit it off and developed a great friendship and mutual admiration. Ken so liked my father's ideas that Ken invited Dad to put together a radio program that Dad calls *Reflections*. Each reflection consists of a story, an idea, or a word of wisdom that is worth thinking about, pondering, and even living by.

Listeners found *Reflections* to be intriguing. They began to report that they liked having this food for thought that they could listen to on their drive home from work. But because one minute goes by so quickly, people also started asking if they could have *Reflections* on a CD, so they could repeat their experience.

The result was that we produced the CDs, which people can purchase by contacting KSAL at www.ksallink.com, or my father's website at www.reflections-for-life.com. The next logical step has been to put my dad's Reflections in a book.

I mentioned that these are ideas that my father tries to live by. He would be the first to tell you that he hasn't always found living by these ideas to be easy. Dad has several degrees, but he considers his diploma from the University of Hard Knocks to be the most important. I think that the thing that has meant the most to my brother and me is that when Dad makes a mistake, or fails to live up to these important ideas, he will be the first to admit it. He will also try his best to improve, always using these ideas as the measure for his own improvement and growth. I think that this is why people have found *Reflections* to be helpful. They speak for themselves. Or, as my father would say, they are self-authenticating.

Many people will find that the nicest thing about *Reflections* is that they are short. Each one can be read in less than a minute, and they can be read in any order. Each one stands on its own, and each one provides nourishment.

The other thing that Dad does not talk about in *Reflections* is that he has written several other books. They take the kinds of ideas that are in *Reflections* and dig deeper. And like *Reflections*, although Dad's other books are about big, important ideas, his books are not difficult to read. Dad writes for laypeople, not for specialists. My prejudice notwithstanding, they are good books! And instead of profiting directly from book sales, Dad gives the proceeds from his books to student scholarships at Kansas Wesleyan University.

Time for Reflection

So why on earth would you move from San Diego, California, to Salina, Kansas?

I get asked that question a lot. People seem surprised. Is San Diego a beautiful place? Yes. Do I have anything against San Diego? No, I don't. And if truth be known, the weather in San Diego is quite mild, and that is true year round.

So what's the attraction to Salina? There are lots of things I love about this community. One of the most important is that Salina is a great place for reflection.

When I was growing up, there was a park near our home. It wasn't quite as beautiful as parks like Sunset or Oakdale, but it was still lovely. We went there to play baseball, basketball, and football. We also ran over its rolling hills. But when we boys played in the park, we would also take time just to lie on the grass, look at the sky, and reflect. Reflection was as important as anything else that we did. It restored our souls. It made us more fully human.

That's one of the main things I love about Salina. It affords the time and place for reflection, and reflection is a big part of living a fulfilling life.

I'm Lost

The man stopped at a service station. He greeted the friendly attendant with the words, "I'm lost."

The attendant was one of those people not easily rattled. His manner was calm and slow. The attendant said, "Well, let's think about this for a moment. Do you know where you've been?"

The man said, "Yes."

"Do you know where you're headed?"

"Yes, sir. I do."

"Well, then, if you know where you've been and where you're going, you aren't lost."

Sounds strange, but it's true. The man felt lost. The problem was that he didn't know where he was at that particular time. So what was the gas station attendant's wisdom?

From time to time, all of us will have that nagging sense that we're lost. We have no idea where we are, and we find ourselves feeling anxious, confused, and even on the edge of panic. It can happen to all of us, and when it happens, it's a good idea to stop and reflect on where we've been and where we're headed. Strangely, this also helps us to discover where we are. When we know where we have been and where we are headed, the fog will lift. We'll find our bearings, and we'll also get to our destination.

Commit First

Have you ever asked the question, what makes a relationship stable and strong? The most important thing I have learned about having strong relationships is that the commitment has to come first. If I put my wife (or anyone else, for that matter) on probation, I will start judging everything that she says and does with reference to the question, "Should this relationship continue?" When I do that, I place her in an impossible situation. Our relationship becomes insecure, and everything we do becomes needlessly strained.

If, however, I say to her, "I am committed to you for life. I will never leave you," then I create a relationship in which she can relax and be herself. She doesn't have to worry about trying to impress me. She knows that she is secure in our relationship. That's when we begin to thrive.

Relationships provide some of life's greatest joy and deepest satisfaction. When our commitment to our relationships is solid, we have a foundation for happiness. Before long, our relationship begins to thrive.

The Molehill

I wasn't a happy camper. When I went to make coffee, I realized that the oven was on. Our daughter had used it the night before, and she had forgotten to turn it off. I was angry, and I told her so. *What a waste! And how can you be so irresponsible? Come on! Use your head!*

That evening, I went into the backyard to light the propane barbecue. The propane tank was empty. The reason was simple: the last time I used the barbecue, I forgot to turn the barbecue off. I wasted an entire tank of propane.

There was only one thing I could do—go to my daughter, tell her what I had done, apologize, and take responsibility. So I did.

Was it easy? No. Rewarding? You bet it was. We both had a good laugh. We both forgave each other. And we both tried to do better at remembering to turn off the oven and the barbecue when we were finished.

What was I doing when I chewed out my daughter for a mistake that I myself was making? I was making a mountain out of a molehill. Neither of us needed that.

Learning from Failure

Failure happens. It happens to all of us. Sometimes we make mistakes. That's because we are human. Other times, we are just plain lazy. Still other times, we aren't realistic. We blow it. We fail. We feel horrible!

What then? I find it helpful to remember that it is human to fail. All of us will fail—at least some of the time. I also find it helpful to *learn from failure*—to spend a little time in reflection, figure out what went wrong, and then make some changes.

Perhaps the most important thing we can do for ourselves is to refrain from beating up on ourselves. After we reflect on the failure, we can let the failure go and try again. The next time we try, we have the benefit of experience that we have spent some time pondering. That's what it means to learn.

A wise teacher once said, "Experience isn't the great teacher. Reflection on our experience is the great teacher."

Have you suffered from failure? Welcome to the human race. Reflect on it. Learn from it. Let it go. And live to the fullest!

A Warm Climate

This wasn't an easy winter. Nor was it an easy spring. We had plenty of snow, which we needed. We then had a week of weather in the seventies. But it got cold and nasty again. And after that, we had flooding and tornadoes.

Finally, the sun came out, and the weather was just gorgeous.

We can't control the weather outside; it is beyond our control. The weather inside is another matter: We can control the weather in our homes—especially when we work as a team. We all know what it's like when the weather in our relationships is stormy, or icy. Who hasn't suffered through a tornado in the home?

The nice thing about the inside of our homes is that we can take responsibility for the climate, and we can do so together. We can use tones of voice that are gentle. We can look at each other with expressions on our faces that are bright and sunny. If we are too hot, we can cool our tempers. If we have been giving each other the cold shoulder, we can give a hug instead.

What happens when we create a pleasant climate in the home? Try it and see!

Two Kinds of Beauty

When I say the word beautiful, what comes to your mind? Is it something that is pleasing for you to look at? That's what I think of first. But there are also *sounds* that I find beautiful. Some things are pleasing to the touch. Are they beautiful as well? How about a well-cooked meal? My wife makes fabulous spare ribs. Can we call them beautiful?

I was reading about beauty. The author said, "Some things are pleasing to look at. But what about things that fit together? Aren't they beautiful as well?"

I am fascinated by that idea. Beauty includes things that fit together well. That means that friendship can be beautiful. When two people ask, "What can we do to fit together, or how can we best work together," they are asking, "What would make this relationship beautiful?"

I love playing piano duets with a colleague of mine at the university. For a duet to be beautiful, our playing has to fit together—hand by hand!

When we think about our relationships, one question worth asking is what can we do *together* that will make our friendship a thing of beauty? The choice is entirely ours.

The Goal of Parenting

Someone asked me, "What's the most important goal of a parent?"

I said, "To prepare the kids to leave the nest!"

My friend looked a little shocked, but I got to explain: "When our children grow up, they need to be able to make it on their own. That means that our job as their parents is to spend the eighteen or so years that we have them under our roof showing them how to live well. And the reason is simple: when they are on their own, they need to be able to live well as well!"

I found that this simplifies matters. Parenting is a tough job. There is no such thing as a professional parent. We are all amateurs under pressure. Parenting involves a lot of improvisation. All too often, we're making it up as we go along.

Every once in a while, it's helpful to remember what we are trying to accomplish: giving our children the capacity to live as adults. Our job is to give them the tools they will need to make it on their own.

Getting Even

We said that we were getting even, but that wasn't really true. When we were small children spending large amounts of time together, we'd get bored. When we were bored, we'd start irritating each other. One of us would tap the other lightly. The one tapped would then tap back, making the second tap slightly harder than the first tap. Then the third tap would be harder still. It wasn't long before taps had become hits, and it wasn't long after that that my little brother would be in tears.

Things always escalated, which meant that they always got out of control. My brother would get hurt, and I, being older, would get into trouble.

That isn't so very bad when we are children, but what about adults? One of the great skills in life is to keep matters from escalating. When two people are together for long periods of time, there will eventually be conflict. Conflict is inevitable. I've found it helpful to reflect back on childhood. When we are children, things escalate, and people get hurt. Now that we're adults, this need not happen. We can see to it that cooler heads prevail.

St. Paul said, "When I was a child, I spoke like a child, I thought like a child, I reasoned like a child. But when I became an adult, I gave up childish ways." Cannot we do likewise?

Getting Unstuck

We received a call from our daughter. She had just rented a U-Haul truck to move some things. As she drove, the entire truck was shaking. It reminded her of those earthquakes we suffered when we lived in California. Needless to say, she wondered what the problem was. Finally, she noticed. She had failed to release the parking brake. So she corrected that problem, and the truck ran smoothly.

Our friendships are like that. We can get stuck. Things then go from bad to worse, especially if we don't know how to release that pesky brake.

So how do we release the brake? How do we get unstuck?

We've found that we can get unstuck when we refrain from overreacting and when we forgive each other. Overreacting is a danger that all of us face. And just as it's human to overreact, it's also easy to carry a grudge.

When we stop overreacting, and when we forgive each other for our human foibles, not only do we release the parking brake and get unstuck, but we get ourselves back on track. That also helps us to start *running on all cylinders*. What a difference that makes!

Success in All of Life

"What does it profit a person to get straight As in college and still flunk life?" Walker Percy is the man who asked that wonderful question. I think it well worth pondering.

One of the reasons I enjoy teaching is that I have wonderful colleagues. They all want their students to do well in the classroom. Even more importantly, they want their students to do well *outside* the classroom as well. They want them to be successful in all of life—in their jobs, with their friends and loved ones, and at leisure.

So what's involved in living a successful life? Do we need to make enough money and save for the future? Certainly. Do we need enough time for rest and play? Of course. What about relationships? What about the ways that we treat and interact with others? What does it take to succeed in the places that count the most?

Doesn't it help to be loving and joyful? What about fairness and honesty? I've never met a person who doesn't like being treated well.

So what does it take to do well not only in college but in life? For me, love, joy, kindness, and honesty are essential. They lead to success that lasts.

Learning to Ride

I was walking in a park. A child was on her bicycle. She was going downhill, picking up speed, and heading straight for some bushes. Then along came three family members who were chasing her. It was then that I realized what was happening. The girl was learning to ride a bike, and her family was trying to help.

What happened was fortunate: The girl rode straight into some bushes. The bushes not only brought her to an abrupt stop, but her momentum pushed her deep enough into the bushes that when she stopped, the bushes held her bicycle in a standing position.

The girl was unhurt, and when her family arrived, all they had to do was to extract the girl and her bicycle from the bushes and move on to the next lesson—brakes.

The little girl wasn't the only person learning that day: So was I. I got to see that learning takes time. There are several steps to learning. Learning often begins as a group effort. And perhaps most important, it is essential to know how and when to put on the brakes.

Spilled Grape Juice

He was three years old at the time. Our son had taken a pitcher of grape juice out of the refrigerator, gone to his seat at the kitchen table, and tried to fill his cup. When he poured, the lid came off the pitcher, and the juice spilled everywhere, including on his chair.

David then got a paper towel and more or less cleaned up his mess—less than more, actually. Since his seat was still wet, he went to the other end of the table, to his sister's seat, and tried again. The result was the same: grape juice went just about everywhere except inside his cup. As I happened to walk through the kitchen just as this second accident was unfolding, Dave looked at me and said, "This is the worst day of my life."

I laughed, and I wished that it would be so. I then got to thinking. Sometimes, it's awfully easy to get upset over spilled grape juice. The truth of the matter is that it was *only* spilled grape juice. It was no big deal—nothing to get upset over. It's all a part of growing up and learning to become a grownup.

Times of Dryness

Every once in a while, our performance is just what we hope for. A colleague and I play piano duets. It's a hobby of ours. On a Sunday afternoon, my wife and I hosted a dinner for family and friends. After the meal, my friend and I tickled the ivories. Our playing wasn't perfect, but it was the best we had done.

The next day, we sat down to practice, and my playing was the worst imaginable. Nothing was satisfying, and I was totally frustrated.

Life is like that. By the grace of God, we have great days. We're on top of our game and on top of the world! Everything unfolds like Springtime.

Those wonderful days are often followed by times that are more difficult. The truth is that times of dryness and difficulty are every bit as important to our growth as the good times. These are the times that test our commitment and our willingness to persevere. When we persist through periods of dryness, we become stronger people and better human beings.

You are Essential

It was one of the most comforting insights I have ever known. It came from a friend. It hit home, and it rang true.

The insight was this: *You are essential.* You have a role to play in life. The role is significant. It is immeasurably important. No one can play that role but you. You are essential to what God wants to happen in this beautiful world in which we live.

I can put it another way: You count. You yourself are immeasurably important. There is one, and only one, you. Your worth is beyond measure. It cannot be calculated or co-modified. You are absolutely precious. Your dignity is sovereign.

Every once in a while, I hope that you will stop and ponder this important truth. I hope you will let it sink in. Not only do you count, but you are also essential to what is supposed to happen in this world.

Balance

I've been blessed with a healthy spontaneity gene. Spontaneity isn't second nature with me; it's first nature: I was born with it! I'm one of those people for whom new thoughts and ideas come easily.

Over the years, I've learned that none of us can live by spontaneity alone. It's one thing to think up a new idea. The difficulty is in what follows. It's important (and I've learned this the hard way) to take a second look at what comes to mind spontaneously. Not every idea merits action. But some things do, and those involve follow-through. Implementation is the hard part. This is what takes both planning and persistence. When I plan carefully and then see things to their conclusion, great things can happen.

In some respects, life is like riding a bicycle. It's all about balance and forward motion. The two things I try to keep in balance are spontaneity and stick-to-it-ive-ness! If I am *only* spontaneous, I can be reckless. But if I only persevere, I can get into a rut. When I manage to balance spontaneity and follow-through, that's when I move forward, make progress, and actually help others.

Making Failure My Friend

Failure. It's one of those constants of the universe. It happens to all of us. No one is immune. It scares us. And it's a part of life. No one goes through life without it.

Failure brings us to a crossroad. It confronts us with a decision: we can learn from it, or we can repeat it—over and over.

Since failure is inevitable, learning from it is the better choice. I have to remind myself (again, over and over!) that experience isn't the great teacher. The great teacher is *reflection on experience.*

When we fail (not if!), that is the perfect time for putting on the brakes and thinking about *what* happened and *why*. What we don't want to do is to repeat the behavior that led to failure. It's much better to make failure our friend. It is as simple as asking, what does this failure have to teach me? What did I do wrong? What can I change? What can I do better the next time?

We're all human. Being human, we will fail—some of the time. Because we are human, we have the capacity to reflect on our experience and to implement change. When we make those important changes, we grow. That's when we become more fully human. Everyone benefits.

Shrunken Man

Haze was in a museum, looking at a mummy. The mummy was a strange figure to behold. It was shrunken and compressed. When Haze bent down to look at the shrunken man's face, he saw his own face reflected in the glass that encased the mummy.

Haze Motes is a character in one of Flannery O'Connor's novels. O'Connor was showing us that Haze had the opportunity to recognize his own shrunken-ness as a human being, which he saw reflected in front of him.

Haze is one of those characters who are small minded, petty, and myopic. His view of life is narrow. Haze lives for himself and nobody else. His life is incredibly lonely. Like the mummy in which he sees his own reflection, Haze is a shrunken man.

O'Connor's story poses a challenge: What would it mean for us to rise to the full stature of our humanity? What would it mean for us to stand tall? How do we go about living lives that are worthy of our dignity as human beings?

Isn't our greatest challenge to live with awareness and the greatest of love? Are we not at our best when we bring joy into the lives of others? And when we live with great love, doesn't that make us more human?

Angels Take Themselves Lightly

"Angels fly because they take themselves lightly." G. K. Chesterton wrote those words back in 1908. What I love about them is that they point out what happens when we take ourselves too seriously: We weigh ourselves down. When I take myself too seriously, it's as though I am wearing a ball and chain, or an anchor. I act as though I am the center of the universe, and everything should revolve around me—my feelings, my priorities, what I want! When I take myself too seriously, I become paralyzed. I create my own inertia, and I get stuck.

Every once in a while, I stop taking myself so seriously. I become less self- absorbed and better able to give my attention to others or to the task at hand. That's when life starts going well. It isn't too very long before I recover momentum and start moving forward.

When I take myself too seriously, I am an unhappy camper. And my mood affects everyone else! But when I stop taking myself too seriously, others start to enjoy my company.

"Angels fly because they take themselves lightly." Aren't these words that are well worth living by?

Twenty-four Hour Test

A rabbi once asked his congregation if they could go for twenty-four hours without badmouthing someone. "Could you live for an entire day without saying something bad about others to their faces, or behind their backs?"

He then said, "If you couldn't go for twenty-four hours without a drink, I'd say you were addicted to alcohol. And if you couldn't live for a day without a cigarette, I'd say you were addicted to tobacco. So if you can't go for twenty-four hours without badmouthing others, are you addicted to critical or hurtful words?"

It's a sobering thought. It's also a wonderful challenge. Can you spend the next twenty-four hours speaking well of others? Are you willing to give it a try?

Wonder

G. K. Chesterton said that the world doesn't lack for wonders, but that people lack a sense of wonder. What is this wonder that he was talking about?

Wonder is a sense of curiosity combined with the feeling of awe. I remember a particular flight to London. I had a window seat on the left side of the plane. Half way across the Atlantic, the pilot told us that if we looked out the window, we would see the Aurora Borealis. This was a dream come true. For the next couple of hours, instead of trying to sleep, I simply looked out of the window, drinking it all in.

Have you ever noticed a child before a flower, or with a new toy? The child enters a new world—the world of wonder. This is what leads to new discovery. A sense of wonder helps us grow to the full stature of our humanity. It also fills us with joy.

Productivity

I met an organic farmer. His work fascinated me. He was also one of those delightfully open and hospitable people. He was never in a rush. He took time to visit. This man was truly interested in what other people thought and felt.

When we turned to the subject of farming, I asked him, "How do you measure success?" I will never forget his answer. He said, "By the productivity of the soil. If my farming techniques enhance the soil, increasing its productivity, then I know I have been a successful farmer."

What an astonishing concept! What if we took his measure of success and applied it to relationships. What if we were to ask, "How can I treat other people so as to enhance their humanity and their capacity to love?" Wouldn't our loved ones be happier? And wouldn't we have a better world?

Loving the Right Things

Have you ever asked yourself, "What is the secret of living a good life?" St. Augustine was one of the giants of western civilization. He lived during the fourth and fifth centuries. He spent most of his life reflecting on this question. He discovered the answer to this question by asking another question: "How do I love the right things in the right way?" For St. Augustine, this was the sixty-four dollar question.

It's a great question. Whom am I supposed to love? And how am I supposed to love them? Where do I begin?

I've found that it's best to begin with those people I'm closest to, the people with whom I spend the most time. For me, this will be my wife, our children, and my co-workers.

How, then, do I go about loving them? I can try treating them as I would want them to treat me. I can also ask them *how* they want to be treated and then do my level best to deliver.

As I try to love others and to love them in the right way, I become a better person. That is its own reward.

Getting Over Ourselves

A couple of days after the San Antonio Spurs won their fourth championship, their coach said something that really caught my attention. He said that the team has a certain character because these are people who "have gotten over themselves." I love that line. These aren't players who are concerned about their own egos or their own playing time. They are concerned about the team and its success. Period.

In fact, when the Spurs were struggling earlier in the season, Greg Papovitch told them that he had no intention of trading them. They were in this together. All that mattered was that they play as a team.

I got to thinking how much we can accomplish and how rewarding life can be when we "get over ourselves" and work as a team. What would it be like for me to make the success of the group at least as important as my own success?

Rooted in the Earth

My favorite part of Homer's *Odyssey* comes at the end. After twenty years, the hero Odysseus is finally reunited to his family. When he arrives home, Odysseus and his wife Penelope don't immediately rush into each other's arms, as we might expect. They first take time to make sure that their relationship is intact and their intimacy is authentic.

Homer then tells us something that I find utterly fascinating: One of the posts of Odysseus and Penelope's bed is a tree that is still rooted in the earth. Their marriage bed can't be moved. It is completely stable.

That is a stunning insight: What makes Odysseus and Penelope heroic is that their marriage bed is rooted in the earth. They know that they can count on each other. Their commitment to their relationship can't be shaken. To put it another way: their home life is rock solid and unshakeable.

Sudoku

Okay, I'm hooked. My daughter gave me a book of Sudoku puzzles, and I love them. They are not only addicting; they can be exhilarating. They can also be aggravating. Sudoku is usually great entertainment, but it is also teaching me something about myself.

First, learning takes time. When I can't see an answer, I am sometimes better off leaving the puzzle and returning to it later. I can then look at the problem with fresh eyes. More often than not, I can then see the answer that was right in front of me all along.

Second, I tend to make mistakes when I am tired. It's harder to concentrate. That means one thing only: it's time to rest.

Finally, one clue, one answer can be the key that unlocks the entire puzzle. Why is that? Because every choice has consequences! Every choice that I make affects the other choices that I make later on. I find this to be true in all of life.

Maddie and Gus

Their names are Maddie and Gus. They are our French Bull-dogs. We also have an English Bulldog named Lady. Lady likes to cuddle; Maddie and Gus like to go for walks.

Their styles of walking are completely different. When we leave our home and head toward the university, Maddie takes the lead. She's the adventuresome one. With her, it's full steam ahead. Not so with Gus. On the trip out, he is all over the place.

When we then head for home, things are completely different. Gus takes the lead. He tugs at the leash; he can't wait to get home. Maddie, on the other hand, follows. She likes to linger.

One day, I realized what their behavior is all about. Maddie is the curious risk taker. She likes to explore all things new. Gus, on the other hand, is a homebody.

Our human relationships are like that. We are all different. And that's why life is so interesting.

Eisenhower

Stephen E. Ambrose is a biographer of President Dwight Eisenhower. Ambrose wrote that by 1952, the year that Eisenhower entered politics, his character was set in concrete. Eisenhower had spent so much time reflecting on his experience that he was firmly established in qualities such as "love, honesty, faithfulness, responsibility, modesty, generosity, duty, and leadership." In addition, Eisenhower had also grown to hate war. Ambrose tells us that Eisenhower was sixty-two years old, and these virtues were *bedrock*.

One of the things I love about Kansas is that people here have a deep appreciation for Dwight Eisenhower. In many respects, he is a wonderful role-model.

But what if we aren't quite where Eisenhower was? What if we, too, want to grow in our character? There's a traditional saying that says, "Sow a thought, reap an action; sow an action, reap a habit; sow a habit, reap a character; sow a character, reap a destiny." That's a thought worth pondering. In time, like Ike, we position ourselves to establish character that is bedrock.

History and Learning

Why study history? Why learn? Winston Churchill said, "The further backward you can look, the farther forward you can see." In the same vein, Goethe wrote, "He who cannot draw on three thousand years is living hand to mouth." What was it that these two great thinkers saw?

There's an old adage that says history always repeats itself. We are doomed to make the same mistakes over and over. Churchill and Goethe recognized that this need not be the case. If we will take time to read, if we are willing to become life-long learners, we will encounter ideas and knowledge that merit reflection. We find something nourishing to chew on. When understanding and reflecting on the past then become a matter of habit, we have placed ourselves squarely on the road to wisdom. When those inevitable challenging circumstances then present themselves, instead of being a part of the problem, we can be a part of the solution.

Churchill also said, "How easily people could make things better than they are—if we only tried together!" This is especially true when our togetherness involves learning, reflection, and the willingness to make changes that benefit everyone.

No Pain, No Gain

Have you heard the saying, "No pain, no gain."? It isn't one many of us enjoy. But in 1899, William James, speaking to a group of teachers, told them that every day they should do something difficult. He said that this is important because we will inevitably face a test, and we need to be ready. If we habitually seek comfort, we will become lifeless and unprepared to face the challenge. And when we are unprepared for the challenge, we find it all but impossible to live the good life.

James told the teachers that habitually doing little things that are difficult is like paying insurance on our homes and vehicles. The payment does no good at the time. In fact, we may never use the insurance. But it may be the very thing that saves us from ruin.

William James said that this is also true for the person who has formed daily habits of concentration, energetic action, and conscious decisions—including the discipline of denying ourselves things that are unnecessary. This is the person who will stand like a tower of strength when everything else is rocking or falling apart.

The truth of the matter is that when we welcome our fair share of pain, we have everything to gain. The most important gain is our humanity.

Fork in the Road

"If you come to a fork in the road, take it!" Yogi Berra said those words. It's a wonderful statement because it causes us to say, "Wait a minute? How do you take a fork in the road?" It's the same situation that Dorothy faced on the Yellow Brick Road.

The important question, of course, is how: how do you take a fork in the road?

I find it helpful to spend ample time thinking about the *kind* of choice I face. Is it a choice between right and wrong, good and evil? If so, then the choice is pretty clear. But what if the choice is between goods? Many of the decisions we must make are like that. We can sure get ourselves worked up over choices of mere personal preference. Perhaps if we simply recognize that a choice between two good things is a good thing, we can choose and move forward.

The simple truth is that life is full of choices—each and every day. Choices lie at the heart of our humanity.

So! If you come to a fork in the road, take it!

Grown-up Talk

"Why don't you run along and play; we're going to have a little grown-up talk."

Have you ever heard that line? Its purpose is to dismiss the kids so that they won't hear what we're about to talk about. More often than not, our motive is honorable: we wish to protect our children, and that's not a bad thing!

But there's a paradox: If we send our kids out of the room every time we talk about important matters, how are they going to learn how to reflect in a grown-up fashion? If we habitually send them from the room, aren't we communicating that we don't trust them? And if they don't learn how grown-ups think and act from us, won't they begin looking to others for an answer?

I don't for a minute think that we want our children to overhear every single thing that we say to each other. But if they are to learn to think, reflect, and act as good citizens and mature adults, I think that they need to overhear model grown-up behavior from us. Moreover, when our children are present as we deal with difficult matters, we are likely to be our best selves!

Action

"I never worry about action, but only about inaction." Winston Churchill said those words. They are a great help to me for one simple reason. I recently spent considerable time making plans. I thought about changes I needed to make. I also pondered things that I needed to get done. I came up with pretty clear plans, and I felt good about my reflections.

But for me, reflection is the easy part. After reflection comes implementation. I've discovered that I can have the best plans in the world, but if I don't implement those plans, nothing significant happens. As my grandmother was wont to say, "I have to get up off my blessed assurance and do something!"

Is reflection important? I think it's essential. But if I don't implement my plans, nothing good happens. That's why Churchill's words ring true: "I never worry about action, but only inaction."

He Was Trustworthy

"People trusted him for the most obvious reason—he was trustworthy." That's what Stephen Ambrose wrote about Dwight Eisenhower.

President Roosevelt once pressured Eisenhower to get tough with the French government. Eisenhower refused. He explained, "My whole strength in dealing with the French has been based upon my refusal to quibble or to stoop to any kind of subterfuge or double dealing."

The result was that when Eisenhower spoke to the French government, they believed him. The reason? He was trustworthy. He wasn't calculating, duplicitous, or manipulative. He aspired to be as honest as honest can be.

Honesty and trustworthiness are two things we can never have too much of. What if people are able to say about us what they said about Dwight D. Eisenhower: "People trusted him for the most obvious reason—he was trustworthy."

Responsibility

"It is our responsibilities, not ourselves, that we should take seriously." Peter Ustinov made that insightful statement. Have you ever noticed how difficult life becomes when we take ourselves too seriously? And have you ever asked yourself why?

One of the reasons is that it isn't pleasant to be around people who take themselves too seriously. They make themselves the center of the universe, and they make their own egos and talents the measure of all things. People who take themselves too seriously act as though *they* are The Almighty.

At the same time, there is a positive side of Ustinov's statement that is every bit as important as the negative: It is our responsibilities that we should take seriously. When we take responsibility for ourselves, we are more pleasant to be around. When we take our fair share of responsibility for life, we aren't burdening others needlessly. In fact, when we take our responsibilities seriously, we complement the dignity of others.

Example

"Example isn't the most important thing; it's the only thing." Albert Schweitzer made that observation. He knew that it is one thing to get on our soapbox and to tell others what they *should* do; it is quite another simply to live by example.

One of the things I admire about people like Albert Schweitzer and Mother Teresa is that they didn't say, "Look at me." They didn't call attention to themselves. They didn't make themselves the center of the universe. They were servants. They devoted their entire lives to serving others.

As a result, people like Albert Schweitzer and Mother Teresa don't become celebrities; they become heroes. They don't talk the talk; they let their actions speak. Because they lived with such great love for others, they became great examples by making our world a better place.

"Example isn't the most important thing; it's the only thing." What if we were to make our deeds our words?

Rights and Responsibilities

"To have a right to do a thing is not the same as to be right in doing it." G. K. Chesterton made that penetrating observation. He knew that human rights are essential. A life without rights is an assault on human dignity. But Chesterton also recognized that people who insist on merely exercising their rights inevitably end up doing the wrong thing.

During the student revolution of 1968 in Paris, there was a slogan on the walls of the Sorbonne that said, "It is forbidden to forbid." Have you ever asked yourself, what happens if everything is allowed? Utter chaos. If I habitually insist on my rights, I can end up doing a lot of damage.

So what's the secret to doing the right thing? It has to do with asking, what's my responsibility? How can I fulfill my responsibility with the greatest love and the greatest joy? "To have a right to do a thing isn't the same as to be right in doing it." If, on the other hand, I habitually ask, "What's the right thing to do here?" I position myself to do just that!

Insatiability

Max Gunther said that the person most likely to grow very, very rich is the person least likely to enjoy it. Why would he make such a claim?

If we are to be happy, we have to have the capacity for satisfaction. But if we are insatiable, we will not be happy because we will never enjoy anything.

Where does the curse of insatiability come from? Insatiability comes from not having a clear definition of enough. If I think I've always got to have more, I am programming myself to be dissatisfied with what I have.

One of the greatest gifts we can give our children is a definition of enough. What does it mean to have enough money, enough food, enough time, and enough toys? What will it take for us to enjoy what we already have?

If we give our children an understanding of enough, and if we help them enjoy what they have to the fullest, we place them squarely on the road to fulfillment.

So, what's enough for you?

Anything Worth Doing

"Anything worth doing is worth doing poorly." G. K. Chesterton said those words. His insight was that perfection is a trap. If I have to do everything perfectly in order to enjoy what I do, I place myself in an impossible situation.

That's because all of us are human. And being human, we are imperfect. We *will* make mistakes. They are a part of life. What do we do with the mistakes that we will inevitably make? Well, we can *learn* from them. Some mistakes have something to teach us. We can also *accept* that we will make mistakes from time to time. That's human, too. Perhaps most important, we can enjoy what we do and do it to the fullest.

One of my hobbies is playing the piano. I love it. Or at least I love it when I'm not too hard or demanding of myself. Music is something for me to enjoy. Sometimes I get it just right. More often, I don't. Most important is for me to enjoy what I do.

Anything that is truly worth doing is worth doing poorly.

Illusions

"It is no use dealing with illusions and make-believe. We must look at the facts. The world . . . is too dangerous for anyone to be able to afford to nurse illusions. We must look at realities." Winston Churchill spoke those words. He was big on recognizing what's truly going on in the world. If we are to live effectively, we have to see what is actually happening right before our eyes.

For Churchill, although facts are essential, this doesn't mean that we must live without hope. He said that "the message of dawn is hope." We have to cultivate hope—day by day. We just can't afford to ignore the facts at the same time. Facts are essential. They help us orient ourselves and find our bearings. They tell us where we are and what is happening. When we face the facts, we clearly know the circumstances in which we cultivate hope.

Our need for hope has never been greater. Hope breathes new life into the most difficult of circumstances. However, nothing will render hope ineffective more than our stubborn unwillingness to face the facts.

Spending Our Lives

Have you ever asked yourself what you want to live for? We have the gift of life. Each morning is a new day. The sixty-four dollar question is what will it take for me to live this day—this hour, for that matter—to the fullest?

William James said, "The great use of life is to spend it for something that outlasts it."

Because I teach, I like to spend the summer reflecting on how I can improve my teaching. I think that the most important thing I can try to do as a teacher is to help my students to ask what they want to live for. What kind of impact do you want to make on those around you? What kind of difference will you make in the lives of others?

One simple way to think about this important issue is to ask, what can I create with my life that will make the world better, and that will outlast me?

So what will it take for you to spend your life for something that will outlast it? Are you willing to do what it takes to leave our world a better place?

Curse and Habit

Michel de Montaigne wrote, "When the Cretans in times past wanted to curse someone, they would pray to the gods to entice him into some bad habit."

They knew that our habits have the capacity to ensnare us in such a way that we no longer reflect on our circumstances or reason about the laws that should govern our lives. Habits can make us blind.

Montaigne also knew that habits are immeasurably powerful because we begin cultivating them from the time we are born. We tend to view and to relate to the entire world through our habits.

The blessings of habit include things becoming second nature—easier. The curse of habit is that it can also hypnotize us, luring our best judgment to sleep.

We can best master our lives by developing our habits consciously and deliberately—with goodness aforethought. It takes time—lots of it. But it will be time well spent.

Consequences

We reap what we sow. St. Paul wrote those words. It's one of those inescapable truths. Many religions describe this reality. It's called the law of consequences. Today, we reap the fruits of decisions made and actions taken in the past. This is true for the good decisions. It's also true for the not so good.

The good news is that this is also where our hope lies. Today, we can sow seeds that we will reap sometime in the future. Our decisions and actions have consequences. This means that we can pause, reflect, and ask, what am I reaping today? Is it desirable? Helpful? What did I sow yesterday that led to today's harvest?

Just as important is the question, what do I want to reap tomorrow? In other words, what is the most desirable future?

I can then begin to sow seeds. I can recognize that the decisions that I make today will have consequences tomorrow. I will reap what I sow. All things being equal, tomorrow can be better than today.

The Right Thing

"You can always count on Americans to do the right thing, after they've tried everything else." Winston Churchill made that statement. Was he complimenting us? Well, sort of. We do like the saying, "Better late than never." There's also a lot to be said for learning from our mistakes. When we take time to reflect on our experience, make changes, and then implement those changes, we improve life.

But there's another piece to Churchill's wisdom. An important part of learning from our mistakes consists of developing the habit of doing the right thing earlier. This isn't always easy. In some situations, there are many things to consider. It is oftentimes foolish to rush into a decision. However, Churchill was also needling us for those times when we know what is right, but we do everything we can to try to weasel ourselves out of doing the right thing in the most timely fashion. It is important to develop the practice of doing the right thing in the right way as early as possible.

"You can always count on Americans to do the right thing, after they've tried everything else." What would it take for us to learn to do the right thing as a matter of habit?

Down Time

Not only were my muscles sore, but I was exhausted. Because I was overweight, I had taken up jogging. A friend convinced me that this is the best form of exercise. At first, I couldn't jog a quarter of a mile without gasping for breath. But I kept at it, increasing a little here and a little there. Finally, I reached three miles. That's when I began to feel my age in earnest.

On the one hand, I was exhilarated. Getting up to three miles was no small feat—at least, not for me! But on the other hand, I was disappointed. My legs were sore, and I needed even more sleep. So I consulted a physician friend, who also jogs. He said, "You need to give your body time to recover. You can't jog every day. And when you increase distance, or number of days that you jog, you have to do it a little at a time. Give your body time to recover.

It was a great lesson for me. Everyone needs down time. Everyone needs time to rest. When we work hard *and* give our bodies time to rest, *then* we can improve a little each week.

Delegating Liability

A father is sitting in his easy chair. His young son is standing, respectfully, in front of the father. His father is in the process of imparting one of the great lessons of life: "Never delegate authority; delegate liability."

This scene was portrayed in a cartoon by Mike Lynch. What makes it so funny is that the father is teaching his son to shirk responsibility. Is there a problem? It's always someone else's fault.

It's a great cartoon. It shows us that one of the most important things we can do for young people is to teach them to take responsibility. Our children need to know that we are responsible for our thoughts and our actions—all of them.

What's the best way to teach our young people to *be* responsible? It's by taking our own fair share of responsibility. When impressionable people see us taking responsibility, we are showing them how. We are also inviting them into a partnership of responsibility. This is what makes our world a better place.

Growing Old

"You are only young once, but you can be immature forever." Germaine Greer spoke those words. What do they show us? The importance of growing up.

Isn't it tempting to want to remain young forever? Who hasn't heard a story about the fountain of youth—that water of life that will make us immortal? The problem is that if I try to remain young forever, I run the risk of getting stuck in immaturity. If we persist in attitudes and behaviors that are childish, we squander our happiness. The irony is that those of us who wish to remain young in old age are often the ones who wanted to rush to adulthood when we were youngsters.

One of the things I love about novelist Robertson Davies is that he recognized that if we age gracefully, if we continue to grow with age, we will find that God has saved the best wine till last. We can relish each day of every age with timely wonder. By doing so, we open ourselves to new insight, new wisdom, and new creativity each and every day. That is a large part of what it means to live fully.

Getting There

"There are people who want to be everywhere at once, and they get nowhere." Carl Sandberg wrote those words. When I read them, I felt like he was talking about me.

You see, I'm one of those dreamers. It's easy for me to think of new possibilities and new ideas. There's nothing wrong with that; it's one of my strengths.

But I had to learn, the hard way, that one's strength can also become a liability. The truth is that not all of my ideas are good ones. Nor are all of them wise. Moreover, if I try to implement too many ideas at once—and I have tried this more times than I care to remember—I end up with too many horizons and too many goals. When I have too many goals, I don't achieve any of them effectively. That's when I get bogged down.

The truth is that I can't be everywhere at once, and I can't do everything at the same time. I have to make choices. Then I will get where I want to be.

Do It!

I once read that novelist Sinclair Lewis was scheduled to give an hour long lecture to a group of college students on the subject of writing. The story said that this accomplished author stood before the students and asked, "How many of you want to be great writers?" Most of the students present raised their hands. Lewis then said, "In that case, I suggest that you all go home and write."

I don't know if this story is historically true, but it certainly expresses an important insight. The most important way we learn is by doing. Practice may not always make for perfection, but it certainly makes us more competent.

There are two things I have wanted to do well—to run and to play the piano. I finally decided that there's only one way to accomplish these two goals. I have to spend time running, and I have to spend time playing the piano.

For me this requires patience and stick-to-it-ive-ness. There are no two ways about it. *I* have to do it. It is *my* responsibility.

Living Fully

Ralph Waldo Emerson said, "Don't be too squeamish about your actions. All life is an experience." I like his advice. Why should we live too tentatively? Life is a gift. Life is a wonder. Each moment is a treasure. So, enjoy. Enjoy the present moment to the fullest.

But there's also a balancing question: How can I get rid of my squeamishness about living to the fullest while at the same time avoid being a panicky cat in a china closet? Robert Louis Stevenson said that "the mark of a good action is that it appears inevitable in retrospect." There is nothing like a good, strong action that is just right for the moment.

So how do we live fully and with gusto? It always helps to spend some time reflecting on where we've been, where we are, and where we are going. It also helps to ask how we can be the most help to others. Am I going to live only for myself, for my benefit, or am I willing to live for something greater, something that will fulfill others?

Habit

Pliny was an ancient Roman. He said that "habit is the most effective teacher of all things."

There's an old story about a woman who lived in a village. When her cow gave birth to a calf, she took the calf into her arms and began to pet it. The woman continued this practice every day. The results were astonishing: by the time the calf had become a fully grown bull, the woman could still carry it.

What does this story show us? Habits develop over time and become incredibly strong. When we make small adjustments in our thinking and behavior, and when we repeat those adjustments day after day, they become a matter of habit. Habits are powerful. In some respects, they express who we are. Most of us live by our habits.

I think that becoming wise involves taking responsibility for the formation and alteration of our habits. And wisdom is one of the most important goals of education.

Negative Thoughts

At the age of twenty-eight, Dominic Grasseth went back to college. At first it didn't go well. He assumed that his teachers wouldn't like him, that he would repeat his previous less than stellar performance, and that he would do poorly.

But instead of remaining stuck in old, bad habits, Dominic took responsibility for his situation. He put the brakes on his negative thinking. He told himself, "If I want to be successful in the classroom, I have to quit being scared."

Dominic became aware of his negative thoughts. Whenever he caught himself thinking that he wasn't up to the challenge, he quickly corrected himself. He also moved to the front of the classroom. He paid careful attention to what his professors said. He kept on track. And he finished the semester with a 4.0.

Upon reflection, Dominic realized that what he had been saying to himself was the underlying problem. At the same time, he realized that what he said to himself could make all the difference in his success as a student. So Dominic made a deliberate decision to speak about himself with the greatest of respect. The result was that his life changed.

I can take responsibility for my thoughts. I can correct negative, irrational thinking. The choice to succeed is entirely my own.

Doing Well

"I wasn't born smart enough. There must be something wrong with me, and there's nothing I can do about it." A group of research psychologists studied the thought processes of students who did poorly in school. This is what they discovered: students who do poorly *think* that they will do poorly and then prove themselves right!

When the researchers looked at students who did well, they found that when these students struggled in the classroom, they would say, "I'm smart enough, so I must not be using the right approach." This second group of students would spend time reflecting on their learning skills and make the necessary adjustments that would allow them to do better in the classroom.

The psychologists discovered that doing well has less to do with IQ or circumstances. Doing well has everything to do with active learning. I can do well in life if I will take time to reflect on my situation and circumstances. "What am I doing right? What am I doing wrong? What changes will I make so that I do better?"

Once I realize what changes I need to make, all that I have to do then is to implement those changes. That's when I begin to learn. That's also when I begin to grow as a person.

Learning and Change

"The only person who is educated is the one who has learned how to learn and change." Psychologist Carl Rogers wrote those words. What I love about them is that Rogers has stated the goal of education, and he has done so in one straightforward sentence. We know we are well educated when we have learned how to learn.

Learning is what makes us fully human. For example, the Blackwells have three wonderful dogs. From time to time, we work at *training* our dogs so that they will fit into our home and be happy. But as lovable as our dogs are, we can't teach them how to learn. They don't have the capacity to reflect on life and then to make constructive changes. Much as we love them, the best we can do is to train them in the kindest way possible.

People are different. We have capacities that greatly exceed training. We have the capacity for education. Moreover, we have the wherewithal to take an active role in learning. Not only can we learn; we can also learn *how* to learn. When we know how to learn, then we can make changes that are both wise and beneficial to all.

Capability

"The deepest personal defeat suffered by human beings is constituted by the difference between what one was capable of becoming and what one has in fact become." Ashley Montagu wrote those words, and are they ever sobering.

From time to time, it is important for me to ask, what have I become? What kind of life am I living? Have I become wise? If not, am I on the road to wisdom? And if I haven't yet become the kind of person I am capable of, what should I do?

In these circumstances, I have found that it is helpful to spend ample time in quiet reflection. I'm not suggesting that we beat up on ourselves. All of us have both strengths and weaknesses, and those strengths and weaknesses play a big role in the way we live. When we try to make changes, our weaknesses may not go away, but we can learn to live with our weaknesses without letting them govern our lives.

Perhaps most important, we can reflect on what we are capable of becoming. As understanding begins to form in our imaginations, then each day we can change and grow, one step at a time.

Gold Medal Battles

In the 1936 Olympics, Jesse Owens won four gold medals. When Owens later reflected on his success, he said, "The battles that count aren't the ones for gold medals. The struggles within yourself—the invisible battles inside all of us—that's where it's at."

I think that Jesse Owens knew what he was talking about. All of us fight battles. Most of the important battles are on the inside. If we are to live meaningful, rewarding lives, we have to look at our willingness to take responsibility, to manage our strong emotions, to pursue meaningful dreams and goals, and to be aware of our attitudes and habits.

Owens knew that it is too easy to see ourselves as victims, or to repeat behaviors that get us into trouble. He also knew that if we are willing to learn from our mistakes, to become emotionally intelligent, and to make active, wise choices, we can win those interior battles and become fully human. Those interior battles are the most important that we face.

Self Esteem

Virginia Satir said, "The foundation of anyone's ability to cope successfully is high self-esteem. If you don't already have it, you can always develop it."

I like Satir's wisdom. We can't control everything in our lives, but we can control whether or not we hold ourselves in high esteem.

For some of us, this is a challenge. I have a close friend whose parents didn't want her to get a big head. To prevent her becoming conceited, they made a practice of putting her down. They taught her to beat up on herself.

It took years for her to recognize that she is in fact a person of genuine, incalculable worth. Does she have weaknesses? Of course. All of us do. But she also has amazing strengths, and she enjoys a wonderful capacity for meaningful relationships and for loving others. By working on her self-talk and self-perception, this person learned to think of herself as a treasure. This is also the way her friends see her.

We may lack self esteem, but we can develop it. It will also give us the capacity to live rewarding lives.

Talk to Yourself

Ken Keyes said, "You must change the way you talk to yourself about your life situations so that you no longer imply that anything outside of you is the immediate cause of your unhappiness. Instead of saying, 'Joe makes me mad,' say, 'I make myself mad when I'm around Joe.'"

These are some of the most helpful words I have ever read. Who hasn't had the experience of becoming anxious, angry, stressed, or scared in certain situations? Ken Keyes recognized that these difficult feelings aren't the final word. We can begin to master these feelings when we think of ourselves as responsible. Instead of blaming someone else for the difficulty I am having, I have found it better to recognize that I get myself worked up in certain situations.

It's even more helpful when I accept that I don't need to continue to get myself so worked up. When I take responsibility for *my* anger, *my* stress, or *my* fear, then I can change. I can get centered, think about what I want or need to do, and take action.

It's all up to me.

The Shoulders of Giants

"If I have seen a little farther than others, it is because I have stood on the shoulders of giants." Sir Isaac Newton wrote those words. He was one of the greatest physicists of history. He's the man who wrote that for every action, there is an equal and opposite reaction. When Albert Einstein later came along, he was able to stand on the shoulders of Isaac Newton, from which Einstein could see farther still.

One of the things that made both Newton and Einstein great scientists was that they recognized how indebted they were to the knowledge and wisdom of people who came before them. They had the humility to give credit where credit was due.

When Oscar Wilde was asked to name the one hundred best books ever written, he said, "I fear that would be impossible. I have written only five." It was more difficult for Wilde to give credit where credit was due.

Whose shoulders do you stand on? Who are the people who have taught you to see? What are the foundations on which you are building your life?

Don't Be Afraid

Do you know what the most frequent commandment in the Bible is? "Don't be afraid." God commands us not to fear more than God commands anything else. Why do you suppose that is?

When William Faulkner gave his Nobel address in 1950, he encouraged us to recognize that being afraid is the most base of human emotions. He said that we should recognize fear and then be done with it forever. Why?

Faulkner said that *fear isn't what makes us great*. What makes us great are the old truths of the human heart—the truths that have been written by the great poets of the Bible and ancient literature. These are the truths not of lust and greed, but of love, honor, compassion, and sacrifice. Our greatness lies in our willingness to embrace the mysterious goodness of God and to be willing to live our lives for something far greater than our petty little quarrels and desires.

For Faulkner, one of the most important things we can do is to read some of the great literature of the past and then try to put it into practice in our lives. The reward is to grow as a person.

Aleksandr Solzhenitsyn

Four years after receiving the Nobel Prize for Literature, Aleksandr Solzhenitsyn told the Swedish Academy that the result of their awarding him the prize was "to prevent him from being crushed in the severe persecutions to which he had been subjected." In other words, by giving Solzhenitsyn the prize, the Nobel committee gave public legitimacy to this courageous hero whose life had been unjustly at risk.

Because the Nobel committee chose to honor Aleksandr Solzhenitsyn, more and more people began to pay attention to him. And because he dared to speak the truth, the truth began to enter the hearts of others. People began to take Solzhenitsyn seriously because they recognized his importance.

Aleksandr Solzhenitsyn dared to tell the truth about the Siberian prisons in which he and countless others had been cruelly incarcerated—without justice, without due process. Because the Swedish Academy chose to honor him, others became willing to hear his penetrating words.

Whom will we honor on this day? Will we honor those who bury us in a blizzard of superficiality? Or will we honor those who sacrifice for the greatest of justice and human dignity?

I Was Wrong

"That was the most significant thing I've seen in my educational career." Those were the words a law student spoke to his professor, Michael Josephson. Josephson had said something during a law school lecture. The problem was that Josephson erred. His words were incorrect, and a student called him on it.

Josephson first considered dancing his way around the issue with a display of verbal gymnastics. Law professors can be pretty good at that. But instead, Josephson said, simply and directly, "You're right. I was wrong." After that class, where the professor openly admitted that he was wrong, a student approached Josephson and said, "That was the most significant thing I've seen in my educational career."

What was so significant? A teacher, whom others looked up to, took responsibility for his error. The student saw someone whom he respected doing the right thing. That made an impact—for the better.

What if we were to do likewise?

Organize Around a Goal

Elbert Hubbard said, "Many people fail in life, not for lack of ability or brains or even courage but simply because they have never organized their energies around a goal." I have certainly found this to be true for me. When I have a goal, I know where I am headed. It becomes easy to set priorities. If something will help me get to my goal, it goes to the top of my list. If something gets in the way of my goal, I get rid of it.

I have the joy of seeing students almost every day. Those who have a clear goal are motivated. Their lives have focus. They not only know what they need to say yes to, but they also know what they need to say no to. Most of our students who say no to the wrong things have a much easier time organizing their energies than those with no clear goals.

So what happens if I have no goal? Perhaps my first goal should be to set some meaningful goals. When that first meaningful goal emerges, our lives have direction.

Before I Die

I learned something from my daughter. She sat down and made a list of all of the things she wants to do before she dies. This includes accomplishments. It includes places she wants to visit (she's already been overseas many times). And it includes the kinds of relationships that she wants to have.

Our daughter is 26 years younger than I am, and she's a heck of a teacher. She got me to thinking: There are several more books that I want to write. There are countries that I still want to see. I want to return to the Louvre in France and the National Gallery in London. I also want to go to visit the Hermitage in St. Petersburg. There are books that I want to read and still others that I want to re-read. I also want to help improve our relationship to the environment. And I want to spend plenty of time with my family. Most important, I want to help others succeed, to get to where they need to be.

What goes on your list? What do you want to accomplish before you die? The time to begin is now.

Resolution to Succeed

Abraham Lincoln said, "Always bear in mind that your own resolution to succeed is more important than any one thing." Was he right? Abraham Lincoln claimed that my ability to take responsibility, my willingness to do what it takes to see things through, is more important than any obstacle that I will face. In fact, if something is worthwhile, if something is important, obstacles are almost inevitable.

There is no such thing as a life free from adversity. There is no such thing as a life that is always easy. There are many reasons for this. It may be that someone else will oppose an idea that is truly beneficial. It may be that something is worth doing precisely because it is difficult. If I only tackle things that are easy, how much will I grow? How much will I strengthen my character?

The things in life that are important require resolve. Things that will help other people draw on our most important capacities.

I am convinced that Abraham Lincoln was right: the most important factor in my mind is my own resolution to succeed.

Superficiality

"Superficiality is the curse of our age. The doctrine of instant satisfaction is a primary spiritual problem." Richard Foster wrote those words over thirty years ago. He was afraid that we spend too much of our time on matters that are trivial, that diminish us as human beings. Foster recognized that we tend to have plenty of toys, plenty of things to have fun with. At the same time, he thinks that we have to little to live for.

What's the solution? Foster also said, "The desperate need today is not for a greater number of intelligent people, or gifted people, but for deep people." Who are the deep people? They are the ones who spend time building strong, healthy relationships. They are the good listeners. They live for the benefit of others. They are lifelong learners. They know that doing the right thing isn't always easy, but they still try.

This doesn't mean that their lives consist of all work and no play. But they do spend a fair amount of time asking, what really matters?

Positioning Ourselves

I asked him the reason for his success. He said, "Getting away from the couch. I have to go to the library." The young man is one of my students. He told me that the subject matter of our class was a bit complex and difficult. Still, he was doing amazingly well. Being a curious sort, I wanted to know why this particular young man was so successful, so I asked him.

He told me that he can't study in his dorm. When I asked why, he said that his dorm room has a couch and a bed, and they are too tempting. Whenever he sees them, he wants to take a nap. He knew that if he were to succeed in the classroom, he had to get away from the couch. So he walks across the street to the library. He may be tired when he arrives, but there are no couches in the library. When he enters the library, his body responds. It's time to study.

What this student does is simple. It is also wise. He gets away from the distractions. He positions himself for success.

More than Required

"Do more than required. Don't do everything allowed." That was Michael Josephson's response when asked the secret of doing the right thing and living well.

When Josephson looked inside of himself, he recognized that it's all too tempting to be lazy, to try just to get by. If I always do the mere minimum, I am conditioning myself to do the least I can get by with.

At the same time, if I always do everything allowed, I run the risk of thinking myself entitled. I am in danger of becoming too demanding. I make myself the center of the universe and expect others to cater to me.

Reflecting on this, Josephson recognized that if we will start doing more than is required, we not only serve others, but we also strengthen our own character. And if we refrain from doing everything that we are allowed to do, we begin exercising more self control.

"Do more than is required. Don't do everything allowed." It's a great way to live.

Just Walk

I wish I could say I walk every day. But when I do walk, I love it. I not only get exercise, but I also listen to great lectures while I walk. It's a wonderful way to renew myself.

But last week, I couldn't walk and listen at the same time. My life had been so busy—running from one thing to the next, solving this problem, putting out that fire, preparing for this class, grading these essays—that I knew I would be better off using the hour just to walk. I needed to empty myself. I needed for all of the stress, anxiety, and weariness to drain out of me. So I spent the hour just walking.

On that particular day, if I had also listened to lectures, or even to music, the walk wouldn't have helped me nearly as much. I needed just to walk. That's all.

Working hard is important. It's a big part of what makes us human. It's also important to help others solve problems, to be there to offer support, and to prepare for the next episode. But at the same time, we have to know when to allow all of the stress to drain out of us and simply to be still.

High Art of Listening

John Claypool calls it *the high art of listening*. It's one of the simplest ways to build strong relationships. He was telling a group of pastors that the best thing we can do for our families is to raise listening to the level of art.

How do I transform listening into an art? If I treasure the person who is speaking, if I truly cherish her as a human being, I can drink in her every word. If I seek to understand what she truly thinks and how she truly feels, then I raise my listening to the level of art.

What gets in the way of my being a good listener is when instead of listening, I am formulating what I am going to say instead. It's even worse if I interrupt. When I do that, I am communicating that what I have to say is more important than what she thinks or feels.

One of the greatest things we can do for the people we love is to give them the gift of our undivided attention. We can be fully present and actually listen.

Which Road?

"One day, Alice came to a fork in the road and saw a Cheshire cat in a tree. 'Which road do I take?' she asked. 'Where do you want to go?' was his response. 'I don't know,' Alice answered. 'Then,' said the cat, 'it doesn't matter.'"

Why doesn't it matter? Because poor Alice had no goal. She didn't know where she was going. She had no idea what kind of person she wanted to be.

Lily Tomlin once said, "I always wanted to be somebody, but now I realize I should have been more specific." This is certainly true for me. For too many years, I wanted to play too many roles and to be too many people. I had to begin to learn that I can succeed only if I start doing fewer things, but do them with great love. For that to happen, I had to ask, where am I, and where am I headed? What's my most important destination?

When we ask that question, then the door will open, and the path will be right in front of us.

It Isn't Where You Came From

"It isn't where you came from; it's where you're going that counts." The great jazz singer Ella Fitzgerald made that observation. Ella, along with most of her fellow jazz musicians, had come from circumstances that were less than desirable. As youngsters, many faced obstacles the size of cities.

But each of the jazz greats had a gift, and each had the willpower not to blame circumstances or to suffocate in the quicksand of pity. Instead, they kept their eyes open and their ears in tune. They never assumed that they were stuck where they were. When a door opened, they took the courage to walk through that door. And when they met other great musicians, they joined in creative jam sessions. They learned from one another. And against the worst of odds, they made some of the greatest music of the twentieth century. They not only knew where they were going, but they got there together.

Ella Fitzgerald is right on the mark. *It isn't where you came from; it's where you're going that counts.*

Our Finest Creation

"Each human life has the potentiality of becoming an art work. To that degree, each of us can become an artist-in-life with our finest creation being our own Self." Ira Progoff wrote those words.

What was his insight? We humans are incomplete, but we also have a lot to say about how we will become complete and fulfilled. We have the imagination and foresight of an artist. The artist has an eye for beauty and an eye for the way things are. The artist also has an eye for what can be. The work of art comes from the mind of the artist. When the artist implements his or her vision, the work of art embodies the artist's deepest insights.

This can be true for any of us. We have the ability to size up our own circumstances. We also have the capacity to imagine what our lives can become. If we then add our own willingness to act on our greatest insights, our very lives can become works of art—our finest creations.

Destiny

William Jennings Bryant said, "Destiny is not a matter of chance; it is a matter of choice. It is not a thing to be waited for; it is a thing to be achieved."

Why are Bryant's words so powerful? He recognized that each of us has a will—the ability to choose. We can *decide* whether to say yes or no. We can give our consent or withhold it. We also have a great creative capacity. We can size up our situations. We can think about where we are going. We can imagine different ways of getting there. And we can act. The choice is ours.

At the beginning of the semester, I asked my students, "What is your greatest challenge?" Most of them said procrastination. "So what will it take for you to stop procrastinating?" The answer was pretty straightforward. "The choice is mine. I'll have to do something." Like Bryant, they were right on the money.

Each of us has the capacity to choose. No one else can do it for us.

Learners Inherit the Future

"In times of drastic change, it is the learners who inherit the future." Eric Hoffer wrote those words, and they have never been more timely.

Scientists with no ax to grind, who live here in central Kansas, have spent a lifetime studying our relationship to the environment. They have thought through questions that will make it possible for our children and grandchildren to enjoy a sustainable future. They see drastic change on the horizon, and they want to help us implement the best of our learning so that the future will hold the greatest of hope.

The alternative would be to stay the course we are on, do nothing, and hope for the best. But this kind of action turns a blind eye to the best that learning affords.

Whenever we find ourselves at a crossroad, we can take a blind gamble, but the important question is where will that get us? Whenever we face challenges—and issues of energy, the environment, and the economy are challenges that are larger than the state of Kansas—will we act on ignorance, or will we follow the best that learning has to offer?

Code of Life

Hans Selye said, "The most important thing is to have a code of life, to know how to live." One of the joys of working in a university is that I spend most of my life with people who actively ask that question. How will I live? How will I love the right people in the right way? Am I going to pursue things that matter, or will I squander my life to the trivial and the superficial?

So what are the things that matter the most? The *Talmud* says, "What is hateful to you do not to your fellowman. That is the entire Law; all the rest is commentary." In the same vein, Jesus taught us to *do unto others as we would have them to do unto us.* In other words, treat people the way you want to be treated.

Have you ever considered what can happen in our world if we will think carefully about how we will live, and if we will then do our best to implement those ideas?

Seeing As We Are

It's tempting to think that we are stuck. When life isn't going the way we would like, who isn't vulnerable to pointing fingers, thinking ourselves powerless, and regarding the situation heartbreakingly hopeless?

The biggest challenge isn't our circumstances; it's our thinking. Anias Nin said, "We don't see things as they are; we see them as we are." All of us face situations that are difficult. What's most important is my view of the situation. If I make a habit of seeing myself as a puppet (a powerless victim with someone else pulling all the strings), I am in danger of accepting circumstances that are unacceptable.

But I don't have to think that way, and I don't have to remain stuck. Instead of pointing fingers or throwing up my hands in resignation, I can size up the situation, see solutions, reflect on the choices that are best, and take action. That's when good solutions begin to emerge. That's also when I embrace greater autonomy.

Forgiveness

"When we confess our sins, God casts them into the deepest ocean, gone forever. And even though I cannot find a Scripture for it, I believe God then places a sign out there that says, NO FISHING ALLOWED." Corrie ten Boom spoke those words to a congregation in Germany in 1947. After her address, a man who had been a cruel Nazi prison guard, with Corrie ten Boom as one of his prisoners, approached her, thrust out his hand, and asked her if she would forgive him of the sins that he had committed against her.

Time stood still. It wasn't something that she wanted to do. But ten Boom had the presence of mind to reflect that forgiveness is not a feeling; it's an act of will.

With the greatest of effort, she forgave the man. It was then that the miracle happened. She says that once she decided to forgive, a healing warmth seemed to flood her whole being. Corrie ten Boom then cried, "I forgive you, brother, with all my heart."

Her experience was that God's grace flowed through her willingness to forgive.

In Love with Myself

"He who is in love with himself has at least this advantage—he won't encounter many rivals in his love." George Lichtenberg, an eighteenth century scientist, wrote those words. His insight is penetrating: If I want to isolate myself from others, I simply need to be stuck on myself. If I think myself superior, if I insist on being number one, I will have fewer and fewer friends because fewer people will enjoy being around me.

What if I were to give up being in love with myself and were instead to take an interest in others? What if I were to live for someone else's benefit, to care about their well being?

When I take an interest in the welfare of others, when I begin to live for someone else's benefit, two things happen. The person whom I care for knows what it's like to be treasured. At the same time, when I begin to care for others, I am changed on the inside. I become a stronger person. I am nicer to be around because I have become more fully human.

Speech

"Speech is conveniently located midway between thought and action, where it often substitutes for both." John Andrew Holmes wrote those words. He recognized that words can be eloquent. They can express the best of intention. Words can express the best of human thought and rise to the level of poetic beauty.

I can know the right thing to do, and I can even articulate what is right. But what if I don't *do* the right thing?

There's a wonderful phrase in our culture: *That person walks the talk*. I can spend time in reflection, thinking things through. In fact, this is an important idea. It is essential for me to spend time in reflection. But once I know what I need to do, I have to take action. I have to implement.

If I speak without thinking, I will help no one. If I spend time in reflection before I open my mouth, I am headed in the right direction. However, words are no substitute for action. The wise are the ones who implement the best that we think.

Eye for Eye

I saw a bumper sticker that said, "Don't get mad; get even." Have you ever asked, what would happen if we made a practice of getting even? Things escalate and then get way out of hand.

Mohandas Gandhi said, "If we all take eye for eye, the whole world will be blind." In other words, if we make it our practice to get even, we will become vengeful, hateful, and destructive. Not only will we hurt others, but our own deepest character will degenerate. We will become less than human.

So what's the answer? When I become angry, I can also be cautious about acting on my anger. I can give myself time to become more centered. I can ask, what will resolve the situation? What action can I take to make things better for the long haul? I can also recognize that I, too, am human, make mistakes, and do things that are wrong. Perhaps most important, I can practice the high art of forgiveness.

It takes far more courage to forgive and to resolve matters than it does to get even. When I get even, not only do I damage others; I damage my own humanity.

The Right Things

In 1978, Aleksandr Solzhenitsyn said, "The difficulties are not imprisonment, hard labor, death, government harassment, and censorship—but boredom, sloppiness, [and] indifference." He also said that we Americans damage ourselves when we make absolute comfort the primary goal of our lives.

So if boredom, sloppiness, and indifference are the problem, what is the solution? St. Augustine said that the solution is to learn to love the right things in the right way. And love is the most noble of human capacities.

How, then, do we get there? By spending time asking the question, what really matters? What are the things that make life meaningful?

I think it has to do with living for something that is greater than myself. I think it has to do with living my life for God, for my family, and for the greater community. If I seek my own happiness directly, I doubt that I will be happy. I think I have a greater chance of happiness if I seek what's best for others.

Time Is of the Essence

One of my favorite authors is Robertson Davies. One of his best essays is on the subject of reading. He said that all of us are given the same amount of time each day. The question is how will I spend that time?

Davies spent much of his time reading. He is one of the best read authors I have read. He read about any subject he could get his hands on. And he did so because he thought reading the best expenditure of time imaginable.

Like Davies, I love to read. I like to spend as many minutes of my day as thoughtfully as I can. But I also realize that I am one person, and your interests may be different from mine.

Regardless of our differing interests, there is at least one reality that applies to all of us equally: time is of the essence. We each get the same amount of time in a twenty-four hour period.

What would happen if you thought of time as a great gift, to be spent wisely? What would you do? How would you live?

Seeking to Learn

"I make an absolute distinction between those who strive with all their might to learn and those who live without troubling themselves or thinking about it." Pascal wrote those words. As far as he was concerned, there are two kinds of people—those who make the decision to learn, and those who either don't care, or who always think themselves right.

Those who learn are the truth seekers. They know that they don't know everything, but they also know that learning the truth is priceless. Truth is what gives us the chance to be just and fair. Truth also allows us to live with integrity.

If I think I know everything, or if I am just plain indifferent and unwilling to learn, I will get stuck in ignorance.

There are things that I can know, and probably should know. The knowledge is there for the taking. But I have to be willing. I have to seek. I have to ask questions. I have to investigate. I have to want to know that truth.

This, incidentally, is what makes us free.

An Open Mind

G. K. Chesterton said, "The object of opening the mind, as with opening the mouth, is to shut it again on something solid."

Did Chesterton recognize that an open mind is essential if we are to live the good life? He certainly did. People whose minds are permanently closed stop growing because they insulate themselves from learning. If I want to become fully human, I have to have an open mind.

But having an open mind doesn't mean that all ideas are equally true or good. If I live by the motto *anything goes*, I will have no basis to avoid what is evil or destructive.

What, then, is the key? Wisdom. If I have an open mind, and if I actively seek goodness, beauty, and truth, then I am on the right track. If I will also nourish myself on what is true, then I will grow. "The object of opening the mind, as with opening the mouth, is to shut it again on something solid."

The Human Heart

It was an experience of great insight. Aleksandr Solzhenitsyn was able to look inside of his own soul. What he discovered startled him: "The line separating good from evil passes neither through states, nor between political parties either—but right through every heart."

Why is this insight important? It is all too easy to think of *my* group as good and *the other* group as bad. We do this with political parties, countries, sports teams, and schools. When I automatically think of someone else as bad and myself as good, it is difficult for me to treat someone else with dignity. It's also difficult for me to improve as a human being.

The truth is that there are good things in all of us, and there are places that each of us can improve. When I am willing to acknowledge my own shortcomings, and when I am willing to grow, then it's possible for relationships to heal and to grow.

The Mission of the Mission

"How do you implement your mission?" That was the first question I asked Steve Kmetz. Ken Jennison, of KSAL, wanted me to meet the Director of the Salina Rescue Mission. Dr. Kmetz's goal is to offer a bright future to men who are homeless, unemployed, and in desperate need of help. So we had lunch together, and I asked how he implements his mission.

He summed up his answer in one word—hospitality. Dr. Kmetz said that his goal is to provide the most loving hospitality possible. He wants the food to be good, the room to be clean, the bedding to be fresh, and the staff to be utterly friendly. The Rescue Mission also has rules, worship, and education. They work tirelessly to give a man the education he needs to live a productive life in our community. But it all begins with hospitality.

Steve Kmetz's goal is that the man who graduates from the Salina Rescue Mission will not only work hard and productively, but will also be hospitable to others. That is a worthy mission.

Learning from Experience

"People don't learn from experience; they learn from reflection and interpretation." Louise Cowan wrote those words. She is one of my favorite authors. Cowan recognized that we sometimes repeat experiences because we make the same mistakes, over and over. When we repeat our mistakes, we usually get the same results—the very results we would like to avoid. To get different results, we have to change.

The key is simple, but it's also easy to forget, especially when we are frustrated and angry. Experience isn't the great teacher; reflection on experience is the great teacher. When things aren't going well, if I will take the patience to slow down, come to a stop, and reflect on what I've been doing to get the results that I don't want, and if I will also make changes in my behavior, I can live a better life.

Easier said than done? Without question. Worth doing? Absolutely.

Under Construction

Flannery O'Connor was once asked why she writes stories about characters who are grotesque. Her response caught my attention. She said that it is easy for us to recognize that the face of evil is grotesque, but it is harder for us to see that the face of goodness is grotesque as well. That seems like a strange thing for a writer to say—until you hear her reason. She said that *goodness is always under construction.*

Her insight is remarkable. Most of us aspire to be good. And any of us who are honest recognize that in spite of our best efforts, we still make mistakes. We are all under construction. Few of us are where we wish to be.

This is a hopeful insight. When we make mistakes, we don't need to beat up on ourselves. We can acknowledge that we are wrong, reflect on what we need to do to improve, and make a second effort—and a third, and a fourth. We are all under construction, and being under construction is a good thing.

Lifted Up

Our need is to be lifted up. Flannery O'Connor wrote, "There is something in us ... that demands the redemptive act, that demands that what falls at least be offered the chance to be restored." O'Connor is one writer who recognized that redemption is one of the marks of our humanity. When broken lives and broken relationships are repaired and restored, everyone wins, and life becomes deeply satisfying.

Why is that? When we take time to be still and to look inside of ourselves, we know, in our heart of hearts, that improving ourselves is just plain good. We don't have to defend improving our lives, and we don't have to defend improving the way we relate to each other. When I take the courage to forgive someone, and when the two of us mutually agree to be more loving, compassionate, and kind toward each other, we both become better human beings.

It is self-evident that redemption and becoming a better human being make life worth living—for everyone.

Kindness

Before he was King Edward II of England, he was the Prince of Wales. And as Prince, he wished to honor a particular gentleman for his distinguished achievements. To do so, the Prince hosted a dinner.

It turned out that although the guest of honor had accomplished much in his service to humanity, his understanding of table etiquette had fallen behind. When the waiter brought tea to the table of the guest of honor, the guest poured the tea into his saucer and drank it.

The future King of England was remarkable for both his insight and his compassion. Quickly sizing up the situation, the King took the tea pot and poured tea into his own saucer and drank it—just like his guest. Other guests, witnessing the King's kind gesture, did likewise.

It is hard for me to imagine a more regal act. The King not only helped one of his subjects save face, but he also taught his subjects to do so at the same time. By expressing kindness, the King taught kindness as well.

Service

His name is Sam Reeve. Several years ago, Mr. Reeve was invited to a Presidential White House Conference on Small Business. Beginning with a small amount of cash, Sam Reeve started a gas station, which grew into the largest service station business in the state of Michigan.

The President of the United States wanted to know the secret of Reeve's astounding accomplishment, so the President asked Reeve. The answer was simple and straightforward: Reeve said, "I try to give away more than my competitors." And what did he give away? Not prizes or stamps or any material reward. He gave service. He cared about his customers. He offered sheer kindness.

Reeve didn't limit his kindness to his business, either. He would shovel the snow from other people's driveways. He would pick up other people's groceries. Whatever he could dream of to make someone else's life easier, that's what he did. That's also why his business grew.

The nice thing about service is that anyone can offer it.

Being Reasonable

George Barnard Shaw said, "The world is formed by unreasonable men. A reasonable man looks at the world and sees how he can fit in with it. An unreasonable man looks at the world and sees how he can change it to fit in with him."

This is a statement I can relate to. In my life, relationships have worked best when I accept people right where they are. This is especially true in our home. If my motto is, "It's my way or the highway," I put others on the defensive and cause needless stress. I fail to honor the human dignity of the person right in front of me, and our relationships rapidly unravel. But when I ask, "What's the best way for me to fit in? How can I honor and respect other people in my family or the workplace?" then the others can relax in my presence. We can find common ground. We can find a place for everyone's strengths. And we can work together productively. That's when our relationships thrive. That's when we become fully human.

Times Like These

One of my students said, "This stuff is hard." I replied, "It's supposed to be. This is college." I have found that college is hardest at the end of the school year. It's difficult to finish strong. People get too little sleep. Those who procrastinate find what they put off catching up with them. And senioritis is rarely limited to seniors.

Paul Harvey said, "In times like these, it helps to recall that there have always been times like these." I tell our students that at the end of the school year, the faculty can be just as stressed as they are. The difference is that we are older, have been down this road many times, and have thankfully developed some skills at dealing with the difficulties of finishing strong. I then remind our students that they are going to make it, and that all of us are in this together.

Life is frequently difficult. Few days are without challenge. It helps to remember that we have weathered difficulty before, and we will weather difficulty again. We, too, can finish strong.

The Cause of Trouble

Bertrand Russell said, "The fundamental cause of the trouble is that in the modern world the stupid are cocksure while the intelligent are full of doubt."

What is Russell's insight? He shows us that stupidity involves being absolutely certain that I am right about something, or that I have all the answers, when in fact I am completely wrong or mistaken. If I think that I am right, when in truth I am wrong, and if I act on my wrong assumptions, then I am in danger of causing trouble—both for myself and for others. On the other hand, I can become wise when I recognize that I don't have all the answers, or don't know all the facts. There may be something significant that I am missing. If I am in that situation, what can I do? I can wait. I can listen. I can open my eyes. And I can let other people know that I have some doubts. There is much that I don't yet know. And I want to know the truth before I take action.

Obligations

Aleksandr Solzhenitsyn said, "It is time in the West to defend not so much human rights as human obligations." Why did Solzhenitsyn make that observation? One of the great strengths of a country like ours has to do with our recognition and emphasis on human rights. We understand that every human being is a gift and merits the greatest of respect. The Bill of Rights is one of the most important documents in all of history.

The problem that Solzhenitsyn recognized is that if I think only of *my* rights without also embracing my responsibilities and obligations, I run the risk of becoming a sponge. I begin to confuse my desires with my rights. I then start thinking of *my* self as entitled to have anyone and everyone serve me—my interests, my desires. When that happens, I make myself the center of the universe.

But if I begin to ask, "What are my obligations?" and if I start fulfilling those obligations, then I can start helping others. And the result is that I position myself to become wise.

Changing Habits

Dostoevsky said, "It seems, in fact, as though the second half of a man's life is made up of nothing but the habits he has accumulated during the first half." Have you ever tried to change a habit? It is one of the most difficult things we can do. Habits have everything to do with the kind of person I am. They are second nature. They are so much a part of us that we speak and act, implementing our habits, without thinking. Habits lead us to say and do things with utter consistence.

The problem is that our habits don't always lead to the most constructive of behavior.

When we then try to change behaviors, things will often go well for a day or two. But when a conflict or crisis rears its head, we tend to revert to our habits.

So what's the solution? We have to be willing to persevere. And we have to recognize that lasting change takes time. We can't be too hard on ourselves. But we can be gently persistent.

The Little Things

Mother Teresa said, "Be faithful in small things because it is in them that your strength lies." I find this to be such a hopeful statement. Mother Teresa knew the secret of lasting change. It begins in little things. By being faithful in something small, I plant a seed. When I follow that up with another small, faithful act, it's like pouring water on the seed I have just planted. When the seed takes root, and I again act faithfully, it's like the shining of the sun on the plant. By then, the plant of faithfulness has begun to grow.

A focus on small things doesn't mean that the big things are unimportant. Mother Teresa recognized that if I am faithful in the big things but compromise on the little things, I will soon find myself compromising on everything. What I *need* is to learn to do the right thing at every level. That means that the little things are as important as the big things when it comes to making right action a matter of habit.

The Right Place

Nasrudin was a figure of ancient folklore. There is a story about the time he dropped his ring in his house. Because the house was dark, he couldn't see. And because he wanted to find the ring, he went outside, where it was light.

A friend came by and asked, "Nasrudin, what are you doing?" Nasrudin answered, "Looking for my ring. I dropped it in the house!" His friend was puzzled. "If you dropped it in the house, why are you looking for it here in the field?" Nasrudin answered, "Because it's dark in the house, and I can't see. Here outside, the sun is shining."

Why was this story important? It showed the foolishness of trying to find enlightenment by looking in the wrong places. I remember how Dorothy, at the end of the Wizard of Oz, made the same discovery. She had been looking for happiness in the wrong place. The truth for her was that happiness lay right where she lived in Kansas.

It never hurts to ask, "Am I looking in the right place?"

Growing Old

"Old people, on the whole, have fewer complaints than [the] young." Hippocrates wrote those words. He didn't mean that as we grow old we are necessarily free from aches and pains. So why would those of us who are older have fewer complaints?

Cicero had the answer: "The great affairs of life are not performed by physical strength, or activity, or nimbleness of body, but by deliberation, character, [and] expression of opinion. Of these, old age is not only not deprived, but, as a rule, has them in greater degree." In other words, as we grow old, what we lose in physical strength is more than compensated by wisdom.

The goal of old age is to become wise. Growing old with grace involves learning to work *together* to solve our problems. It involves understanding when we have enough. It involves learning to use fewer material resources, but using them to the fullest. It involves learning to give—to enhance the capacity of young people for wise living and to enhance the capacity of mother earth as well.

Upon Further Reflection

One of the great additions to the world of televised sports is the instant replay. Years ago, this amazing technology made it possible for the viewer to see the play again and again in slow motion. Years later, the National Football League began to use instant replay as a way of allowing officials to correct mistakes. I marvel at the accuracy of professional officials. They don't miss many calls. But because they are human, they aren't perfect. And in the interest of fairness, I am glad that they have the opportunity to further review their call.

What I like about instant replay is that it is nice when we have the opportunity to review decisions we make and actions we take in real life. This is what the discipline of reflection is all about. When I re-read and edited these Reflections, I was amazed at how much I forget and how important it is that I take the time to review the ideas that I want to live by. For many of these ideas, I felt like I was reading them for the first time.

Simply put, one of the most important lessons I have learned is that I learn best when I take the time to review. I consider myself a slow learner. Moreover, I have learned that learning is a lifelong adventure.

Perhaps most important, upon further reflection, I have learned that the opportunity to review sits firmly in the grace of God. That in itself merits reflection!

About the Author

John N. Blackwell is Dean of the Chapel at Kansas Wesleyan University, where he also teaches in the departments of Religion and Philosophy, English, Behavioral Sciences, and the Honors Program. For over thirty years, John has also been a retreat leader for people of all ages and speaker at numerous conferences.

John received his education at San Diego State University, Claremont School of Theology, and Arizona State University, where he earned a Ph.D. in cultural anthropology. This is John's sixth book.

John and his wife Nancy make their home in Salina, Kansas. Their daughter Jaime, son David, and daughter-in-law Chynnene also make their homes in Salina.

Acknowledgments

Book publishing is not something that an author does alone. There are several people I wish to thank. David Hancock, my publisher, and his staff are always a joy to work with. They conduct themselves as professional collaborators every step of the way.

Philip P. Kerstetter, President of Kansas Wesleyan University, kindly allowed me to offer these Reflections to the listening public on behalf of the university. Phil is not only a most trusted friend; he is a champion of the art of reflection. Every day, it is an honor and joy to serve on his staff.

I take delight in dedicating this small book to three wonderful friends. Shirley Leggett is one of my greatest supporters and collaborators, especially when it comes to the world of ideas. She also serves as my editor and proofreader.

Ken and June Jennison are also kindhearted friends. They may be counted among Salina's strongest and finest citizens, having done much selfless work to make Salina one of the great cities of the Midwest.

This book is but a small token of the great gratitude I feel for Shirley, Ken, June, and their tireless work and support. They also embody the best of the ideas that these Reflections try to convey.

I am also grateful to our daughter Jaime for writing the foreword to this little book. Jaime is a thoughtful champion of great ideas.

Finally, I want to thank my family—Nancy, Jaime, Dave, and Chynnene. Because of their love, each day overflows with joy.

Books by John Blackwell

A Whole New World—the Gospel of Mark: Great Insights into Transformation and Togetherness. (New York: Morgan James, 2007)

A Whole New World—the Gospel of John: Great Insights into Transformation and Fufillment (New York: Morgan James, 2006)

Pride: Overcoming the First Deadly Sin (New York: Crossroad, 2006)

The Noonday Demon (New York: Crossroad, 2004)

The Passion as Story (Philadelphia: Fortress Press, 1986)

Reflections (CD)

If you would like to purchase a CD of Reflections, or any of John Blackwell's books, you may do so by going to Blackwell's website, www.Reflections-for-Life.com, or by contacting him at jblackwell@kwu.edu. All profits from the CDs go to the Dr. John and Nancy Blackwell Family Scholarship Fund for student college tuition scholarships at Kansas Wesleyan University.

BUY A SHARE OF THE FUTURE IN YOUR COMMUNITY

These certificates make great holiday, graduation and birthday gifts that can be personalized with the recipient's name. The cost of one S.H.A.R.E. or one square foot is $54.17. The personalized certificate is suitable for framing and will state the number of shares purchased and the amount of each share, as well as the recipient's name. The home that you participate in "building" will last for many years and will continue to grow in value.

Here is a sample SHARE certificate:

HABITAT FOR HUMANITY

THIS CERTIFIES THAT

YOUR NAME HERE

HAS INVESTED IN A HOME FOR A DESERVING FAMILY

1985-2005

TWENTY YEARS OF BUILDING FUTURES IN OUR COMMUNITY ONE HOME AT A TIME

1200 SQUARE FOOT HOUSE @ $65,000 = $54.17 PER SQUARE FOOT
This certificate represents a tax deductible donation. It has no cash value.

YES, I WOULD LIKE TO HELP!

I support the work that Habitat for Humanity does and I want to be part of the excitement! As a donor, I will receive periodic updates on your construction activities but, more importantly, I know my gift will help a family in our community realize the dream of homeownership. **I would like to SHARE in your efforts against substandard housing in my community!** *(Please print below)*

PLEASE SEND ME _____ SHARES at $54.17 EACH = $ $_____

In Honor Of: _____

Occasion: (Circle One)   *HOLIDAY*   *BIRTHDAY*   *ANNIVERSARY*

      OTHER: _____

Address of Recipient: _____

Gift From: _____ *Donor Address:* _____

Donor Email: _____

I AM ENCLOSING A CHECK FOR $ $_____ PAYABLE TO HABITAT FOR HUMANITY **OR** PLEASE CHARGE MY VISA OR MASTERCARD *(CIRCLE ONE)*

Card Number _____ Expiration Date: _____

Name as it appears on Credit Card _____ Charge Amount $ _____

Signature _____

Billing Address _____

Telephone # Day _____ Eve _____

PLEASE NOTE: Your contribution is tax-deductible to the fullest extent allowed by law.
Habitat for Humanity • P.O. Box 1443 • Newport News, VA 23601 • 757-596-5553
www.HelpHabitatforHumanity.org